No Immediate Remedy

JEAN ANDREWS

THE CHOIR PRESS

First published in the United Kingdom in 2024 by
The Choir Press

ISBN 978-1-78963-423-5

With thanks to Lorna Shaughnessy and Bernard McGuirk,
pathfinders both;

in tribute to Eithne McCarrick,
dear departed mistress of the *aperçu*.

Contents

Infamia

And now?

Notes

Covidia

I - Recovery Suite

1. Krassimira

Libera me

Where did you get that voice?
Where did you summon it from?
Not the fine bel canto instrument,
exquisitely schooled,
bowed by the violinist you once were,
broad-shouldered and monumental
like the greats of the fifties,
and floated at the top
like the many points of the evening star.
No. Not that one.

The other one,
with which you bellowed at,
harangued and stalked your prey,
imperious and implacable,
like Nemesis, as if you were
the justice of the immortals
and Death a cornered transgressor,
trembling and diminished,
cowed at your command,
beneath your enraged Olympian stare,
your *Libera me*.

2. Rivers

los ríos/que van a dar en la mar

The many rivers which we see
flowing slowly, flowing turbulently, flowing reluctantly
into the astounded, heartbroken ocean.
They are not those you imagined
as you lamented a departed father,
gone at a fitting time to meet the maker
you all took for granted in a regulated Heaven.

No, these are usurpers, impostors, unwelcome strangers.
We did not invite them nor expect them
nor do we extend our hospitality
for there should be no inevitability to their coming
and we do not comply with their request.
We do not consign our brothers and sisters resignedly
into their arms since they are not safe, not trustworthy, not right.

3. Heaven, 1918

Als wie in der Mutter Haus

There are lies parents are told,
cling on to,
when their children die.
They are happy, at rest, in paradise,
far removed from their progenitors' pain.

But what can take
from the physical shock of those inert bodies,
suddenly ragdoll floppy, sickeningly cold,
at the instant of the flight of the soul?
Not those fairytales that lulled them into a secure sleep,
nor those dreams long lost in the toil for everyday survival,
not even the hope that theirs would be a better future after
the war,
now vertiginously, unspeakably gone.

Are not the old supposed to go first,
rendered children again by the erosions of age?
Not the rosy-cheeked, curly-haired young,
with every mistake of theirs yet to be made?

4. The Swan at Fuldatal

Mo ghrá thu agus mo rún!

There is no reason why a *coup de foudre*
should result in lasting love,
affection to withstand a new baby year after year
and the same man's wandering eye,
his never-sated desire for conflict.

There is every reason why a wife
would drink his assassinated blood
and keen him in traditional cadence
in the usually observed places,
in prescribed company and at the ritual times.

This is why the swan near the Fulda landed and settled
between the two train tracks, hence enormous delays.
There she would have remained
until her lifelong mate, electrocuted in the overhead lines,
had assimilated fully into the beckoning haze.

But she was uprooted,
taken to the riverbank that very day.
A sacrilege akin
to those pressurised adieus by camera phone,
when patients expiring on a hospital bed
are far beyond the reach of any device
but cannot be afforded
what they had at their birth,
the skin-on-skin reassurance
of family, flesh and bone.

5. Forgiveness, 1941

Elle est tout amour

There is no forgiveness.
Is this because there is no-one to pardon,
no one person to shoulder the blame?
We have all committed errors,
we all had a stake,
some have not survived, will not survive.

When you were a prisoner of war,
it was clear what was amiss
and who had brought it about.
Though, forsaken on the German-Polish border,
it must have seemed there could never be a way out.

But you saw it was not the end of time,
instead, the betokening of a beginning
heralded by that shining angel of *Revelation*.
You stitched together harbingers from a decade before
with new witness etched in that camp
and four of you inhabited
testimony which, in its starkness,
even today stills the listener's heart,
even when we know the end is hope,
begotten, within the darkness,
through compassion and love.

II - Statistics and Collateral Damage

100,000
(26th January 2021, UK total)

A month ago would have been St Stephen's Day,
the first Christian martyr, stoned to death.
It snowed on the equivalent of Christmas Eve
and stayed on the ground in Winter sunshine
throughout the avatar of Christmas Day.

But we are a month into the New Year
and instead of a boy laid in a manger
we have reached a tenth of a million dead.
This has come upon us quietly,
unless one of our own has expired
alone, intubated, isolated on a screened-off bed;

or we are some of those tending the proned
in cots on ventilators, in oxygen hoods,
enshrouded ourselves in latex and paraphernalia,
sweaty and delirious with strain and disbelief.
That it has come to this, blanketed
not in snow but in haphazard grief.

L'après-guerre

Egon Schiele at 28,
gone in an instant in Vienna.
His compatriot Gustav Klimt,
twenty years his elder,
also taken.
Both in 1918,
no bomb nor bayonet in sight.

One of my own uncles,
a mere child,
extinguished the same way.

Over 50 million dead they say.
Two and a half times those taken
in *La Grande Guerre*
but only remembered, if at all,
by their families, one at a time.

Each loss a fine grain of sand,
never counted on a beach,
nor chiselled on a monument of stone.

Everyone wore cloth masks,
then promptly seemed to forget,
once the danger to the young was past.

Joe's 500,000
(22nd February 2021, U.S.)

A man burdened with much grief
who wears it like a fur coat in the Arctic Winter
and a panama hat in the glare of Summer,
knowing its full weight, squaring his shoulders
yet again in a long life, and ready to speak:
the lately-chosen high priest guiding his people
across their multitudinous landscape of tears.

Where he has been and continues to go,
they can follow him, trust his navigation,
let themselves be carried in the long flow
of communal lamentation.

A world which had no time and would not slow,
dismissing heartbreak as indulgent sentimentality,
loving regard as weakness of resolve,
the bonds between lovers or family as fickle ties
best forgotten and easily replaced,
at last brought to a crux of reflection.

These are the capillaries of life itself,
belittled at our peril.

The Living Innocent

An owl stares out of the Twittersphere,
clad in that ominous placard familiar to all of us:
a pleated, blue surgical mask,
hanging by one of its loops
from his golden-feathered neck.

The innocent creature cannot slip out of it.
That flexible hoop sits with sufficient traction
on his patterned, tapered plumes
to damn him to weeks of discomfort and distress,
if not to eventual death.

For all that we need to protect ourselves,
impeding this tawny, nocturnal beast
from food and flight and everyday life
is a far cry from any definition of success.

The Innocent Dead 1,
Lament for a Prince of Greece

The piper paced a slow step,
heel toe, heel toe,
side to side in a sailor's roll,
and the mounting wail of his lament
ceased at the threshold
of a Gothic arch
midway through a repeat
of his rising call.

This was the sometime Adonis'
final request,
a life unfinished, interrupted,
the bagpipes stopped by a hard stone wall,
two months' short of five score not out,
a private, pared-back event,
surreptitious bounty of the pandemic gods.

The Innocent Dead 2

For Dianne

Often, we don't know the calibre of the dead
until they are quite a long time gone.

And they can sometimes return to wish us well,
allow us the chance to express our grief to them,
and not only to their family and friends.

As you did, smiling daughter of the gods,
golden in life and essence and everything else.

You did not want a funeral and all that stilted show.
You lived and your time had come,
you loved and your deeds were done.

I doubt if there are many, especially now,
who could leave this world with such aplomb,
that message to all those left of us:
to live our lives fruitfully, and always to the full.

The Innocent Dead 3

These are not the dead of now
but those who will be soon,
on whose certificate
no breath of Covid will appear
and yet these last two years of life
will show the mark
of pestilence and confinement,
in their shortened term
on a sorrowful Earth
rent by panic and disagreement,
all the failings,
as well as the blessings
of our human state
jostling for a spot in the queue
to get the hell out
of this benighted place.

Ucrania

25th December 2021

Every year there's a moment
when the world stops,
holds its breath,
stills on its axis.

I can't always tell
because that instant is different
for every changing year,
each with its own mood.

I never know
how it will come,
in joy or sorrow,
security or fear.

This time round,
I think it came
with a family of swans
on a very cold lake.

Two cygnets had survived
from nest to mottled feather
and seemed to thrive.
Many times there are none.

Looking back,
now two months gone,
my sunken heart,
to be so wrong.

26th February 2022

A yellow, snub-nosed dog
carried in an old man's arms,
like a toddler worn out from a walk,
looks at us over his owner's shoulder
as the man descends the stairs
into the depths of the Kyiv underground.

Two days in
and this dog is not left to fend
alone in the street,
but he knows.

2nd March 2022

Fedya is old.
A Russian blue
though he has no time
for that sobriquet now,
not while missiles
are coming down
to flatten his ears
and the buildings
all around.

3rd March 2022

Tractors tow
abandoned tanks
like ricks of hay.
Saved to fight
another day.

8th March 2022

They were encouraged to bring their pets,
unlike their great- and great-great grandparents,
forced at a moment's notice from their smallholdings,
from generations of living with animals in their midst,
those in the house and those in the fields,
into the concrete of treeless streets.

This time, nobody would have to leave their cats,
long-haired, square-headed, biddable and sleek,
easy on a harness or sitting in a small child's backpack,
perching on someone's shoulder, draped around their necks,
even when frightened, confident in those human hands
that cradled them beneath down-filled anoraks.

I look at my wayward, tortoiseshell diva
and wonder how we would cope
when she will not even let me pick her up.
She would flee into fear and feral misery,
destitution I had rescued her from before,
rather than trust me to lead us home.

8th March 2022, as well

Horace's ears are so big,
those flying Dumbo flaps
that channel sounds
towards the little bones
inside his noble, wrinkled head,
that he hears everything
many times magnified.

His body is far too large
for shelter underground,
so his keeper sleeps
between his monumental pink feet
and feeds him apples when he is upset,
when ordnance falls from the night sky
on those who have done no wrong.

11th March 2022

She bore her big brown dog,
a German shepherd,
mortified to be slung
fireman-style
over the shoulder
of the owner
whose safety
it once had been his duty
to guarantee.

All of seventeen kilometres,
with a tiny purple rucksack
and her aged Alsatian,
to reach the border.

The camera caught
the old dog's mournful eyes.
We only saw her,
hooded,
long legs striding out,
from behind.

11th March 2022, also

An eight-year-old girl
with her schoolbag strapped
around her front
so she and Valeria, her cat,
could see each other
as the two of them took
the long journey
into banishment.

Valeria's broad blue head
and expression of irked disdain
the only thing
to keep that blameless child
from sinking into
the churned-up terrain.

18th March 2022

Some days ago,
a photo of a man
beside a burnt-out house,
his wife, his son,
his daughter-in-law
and his wife's mother,
all gone.

The only being saved
– he clutched him to his chest –
was his black-and-white tom,
the only one with whom
he had memories to share
of what had been destroyed
by that random bomb.

26th March 2022

A whole heap of kangaroos,
I kid you not,
of many sizes and several hues,
crammed in the rear of a saloon van,
on their way out of Kharkiv zoo.

And cowed as any marsupial would be too
by the giant exploding cones
in this muddy land that is not their outback,
this turmoil amongst the hairless species
that both commodifies them
and strives to keep them safe.

1st April 2022, Two Snipers

He sits on the skeleton of a stairs,
only its stepped profile left now,
in helmet and military fatigues,
crouched over the telescopic sight,
the tip of the barrel just within
the blown-out window frame.

There's no barrier to me here.
I balance my front paws on the wooden sill,
only the cocked tips of my ears might be noticed,
and even then, there's nothing on which to focus.

He's only a human, with limited senses,
my hearing and terrier's snout
will bring more to the battle
than any sharpening of his.

1st April 2022, Target Practice

I sit across the small of his back
while he takes shots at concentric ring targets.
He fires rapid rounds, each rebounding
through his shoulder,
making thunderous noise
in the shooting ground.

I stay where I am, whiskers attuned,
jerking as he does, ears flattened
to block out the reverberation.

I know it seems rather quixotic
but his body is soft and warm
and we depend upon each other.

3rd April 2022

He must have been a mastiff,
as big as the woman embracing him,
velvety brown, ruched pelt, seeming to sleep.

He should have been buried in the forest
with his forebears, his canine clan,
but the enemy laid mines in the undergrowth
and he ended up in a human body bag.

14th April 2022, Tasha

Far away in County Clare
– shaped like a seahorse
facing the Atlantic –
an eighty-six year-old
all the way from the Black Sea coast
waits for her grey-muzzled dog,
left behind along the way
but still alive because her displaced owner
had not the heart to have her put to sleep.

Now she emerges from a cage
in the back of the last of the many cars
piloted by volunteers conveying her west,
diminutive for a Labrador bitch,
bedraggled by the miles she has travelled,
confused by the unfamiliar scents.

She is greeted by cameras
and grey fluffy microphones
thrust in her bewildered face,
this poor exhausted dog
who only wants to rest her bones
on the floor beside her keeper, Violetta's
slippered and swollen, elderly toes.

21st April 2022, Bucha

Sima has been on the run
for forty-five days of the eighty
since the invasion was begun,
since her family became refugees
and she hid in her secret place
where the enemy could not find her.

Their hearts more broken
by leaving her behind
than the loss of hard-won dwelling
and possessions,
now, after a week of calling,
she has emerged,
tattered, saucer-eyed, skeletal.

This bedraggled, purring creature,
folded, at last, in the arms of one of her people,
is the treasure they thought never to recover
on their return to the footprint of their onetime home.

21st April 2022, Sentinel

He is in the operating theatre
to have damage deliberately done
unto his physical self by another human creature
made good or at least passably repaired.

God knows if they have sufficient anaesthetic
or anti-infection drugs,
God knows if the generators will hold
or the wounded man have time to mend.

A rangy, biscuit-coloured dog
stands in the corridor outside the door,
his master's next-of-kin
in this awful iteration of war.

21st April 2022, Kharkiv

I heard a rumour on the news.

Two keepers who remained in the zoo
to feed the captive animals
were lined up in the toilets
at their place of work,
one with a bucket of carrots,
the other a crate of bananas,
and summarily shot.

Caught whilst washing the carrots,
pulling bananas from their stalks,
mundane tasks in the midst of war.

Oblivious parents begat the children on either side
who grew up to think of acting like this.

2nd May 2022

I send kibbled cat food to Ukraine.
Some portion of my taxes
dispatches weapons.

I wish neither were true
and all those long-haired cats
lay on cosy, warm beds,
snoring beside their two-legged friends.

11th May 2022

You think of us as cute,
highly intelligent,
affectionate maybe,
and you like to see us leap,
singly or in schools,
through the undulations of the sea.

You may not know
that we are now as destitute
as all those humans
packed on buses and trains,
forced from our Black Sea home
by the cacophony of missiles,
torpedoes and propeller blades
that has curdled our sonar zone.

That now, we are dying further south,
cast adrift among the fishing lanes.

14th May 2022, Ihor and Zhu-Zhu

A man in his sixties,
a former ship's cook,
like most, a smoker,
useful socially
when captured
by the enemy,
luckily minus tattoos,
says he walked,
along with his dog,
the hundred and forty miles
to salvation,
out of the devastated port,
with fifty kilograms,
what remained of his life,
packed in a large wheelie bag.

At times he carried
the black-and-brown terrier,
her paws sliced open
by shards of metal.
At least once he told her
she had to use them
or they would both
be destroyed.
They caught lifts,
slept where they could,
got through checkpoints
and temporary arrest,
and crossed a ruined bridge,
he, walking on a single wide girder,
she, on a narrow rail overhead.

When he had to,
he downed shots of vodka
though he had given up drink,
removed his shirt to demonstrate
his skin was clean,
in more ways than one,
at every stage held on
to his nine-year old companion
or left her outside to wait
as he endured a further
clumsy interrogation.

An otherwise unremarkable man,
now living with his elderly parents
on no income in the capital.
The little dog is in need of a vet.
He claims to be fine.

This, after their impossible trek
on four lacerated paws
and two determined feet
out of Mariupol,
the port city which had been
both his living
and their life.

24th May 2022

There are installations that look like drainpipes
opened out into large ladles at the bottom.
They are dotted around bombed-out parts of cities
in places where they can safely be installed
and easily refilled with petfood biscuits.
They are for those whose people have been killed
or were forced to leave without them,
and also for their feral kin.
Otherwise they would have nothing
but each other to eat.

You might think
that this is not the most relevant statement
that could be made about an invasion
of which there are
no imminent signs of defeat.

Sorbet

Le choix

A flop-eared, sad-eyed basset hound
or a two-month pup galumphing round?

L'adieu

My cat was killed on the road,
then crawled through her wall-flap
so I would know.

Le rencontre

He jumped from the seventh floor.
She breathed in his last
from the path below.

La réponse

Her text reply,
that things are tough -
pure circumspection,
she's had enough.

Le phénix

A starling careened into the windowpane,
then rose and flew again.

La glace

The next ice age
is eight thousand years hence.
What price progress
in that case?

La trouvaille

Yesterday,
a grey gardening glove
erupted from my petunias.

L'après-midi

A puff-tailed rodent squats in the garden,
sly, shape-shifting antelope.

Le pont

A heron's flight,
galvanising the lips of the ravine
to unite.

Le soir

A flash of fox on an urban street,
places to go, creatures to meet.

Le crépuscule

At sunset,
curled-up mallard,
dotted like jewels
round the man-made lake.

La beauté

Venus traversing,
frolicking cherubs
rolling their *whatever* eyes.

La nuit

I saw a famous man,
long dead now,
give alms
when no-one saw.
He thought.

Le chemin

Late and dark,
a fork in a country lane
and a badger ambles home.

Les feux d'artifice

Fireworks arc in the sky at night,
seraphs on furlough from Paradise.

Infamia

24th May 2022, Uvalde

All that was left.

Her high-top,
green Converse trainers.

After the trigger was pressed.

24th June 2022,
The Other Side is Damnation

I

1. If Jesus were to walk this Earth again
   he would still be a poor man,
   with a visceral distrust of power,
   orthodoxy and bureaucrats.

2. He was kind to women,
   maybe trusted them more
   than their male cohorts,
   who then obliterated the distaff legacy.

3. He understood the suffering of children,
   famously called them unto himself,
   including those brief lives and swift deaths
   imposed by Herod at the time of his own birth.

II

4. The old, the indigent, the frightened, the betrayed,
   these are the bearers of lives forced into being
   by those cushioned in sententiousness,
   driven, who knows by what paranoid creed,
   who live in fear of a capricious Almighty
   and have it that each sperm on its way
   to penetrate an egg must contain a soul,
   the egg and the womb being mere empty vessels.
   They hold that this journey must not be forestalled
   or the wrath of their vengeful God
   will be unleashed, though not for them to bear,

oh no, my dear, vanish that thought,
but borne by each mother and her baby.
Yet, once the miracle of birth has taken place,
if they have not even a manger
in which to lay their heads,
who cares, since in this world
it is every man for his goddamn self.

5. Those women who can only countenance
    the abnegation of animal sex,
    the debasement of proffering
    their shameful nether parts
    as a non-negotiable aperture
    to still the barbaric urge
    of a creature who may be necessary
    to underpin their lives in all other respects,
    cleave to the belief
    that each of those degrading, unpleasant acts
    entails the potential for new life, a sacred thing.
    Otherwise, how can they live
    with what they are doing and have done?

6. In a perfect world, all babies are loved,
    all mothers cherished,
    all conceptions joyful,
    all fathers caring and lifelong,
    but this is not what is ever on the cards
    for a woman who cannot take a pregnancy
    the full nine yards.

III

7. Now the Catholic primate of All Ireland
   is getting in on the act.
   That Godfearing nation across the pond,
   palace of the dreams of emigrant generations,
   has pronounced on its Christian duty
   and we should all rejoice.
   It does not matter that our little nation decided,
   by popular majority and though a process
   of much-lauded consultation,
   to recommend the more compassionate path.

8. And so, because of modern healthcare,
   better nutrition, childhood vaccines, antibiotics,
   vitamins, evolution per se,
   a ten-year-old girl can conceive a child.
   None of her bones are fully grown,
   her internal organs are not at adult capacity,
   her female hormones are barely there,
   the same applies to her sense of self,
   yet there are legislatures in the Land of the Free
   that require that she, perhaps befouled by familial rape,
   should carry the child of her brother, father or uncle
   and undergo the rigours of labour and vaginal birth
   because this will be a salutary lesson
   for the rest of her mortal time on Earth.

IV

In rebuttal, they will argue
that these are extreme examples,
for which there must be sympathy,
but that it must be one law for all
otherwise the moral dam will break.
Except it never is like that
and a raped daughter of theirs
will be taken care of,
with a wadge of cash to the wise
and so forth,
while the salutary lesson
can take the high road
all the way to tarnation
and much, much further beyond.

31st July 2022, Retribution

The thing is,
is it ever right?

A superpower that executes the poor,
the uneducated, the mentally ill
but allows monied exceptions
to every rule.

A people whose defence of freedom
permits the annihilation of their own children
with weapons the use of which
they roundly condemn
in the hands of anyone but a white, homeland citizen.

This jubilation of gaming technology
deployed to assassinate one notorious,
single-minded old man,
seated on a balcony in another sovereign land?
This mindset of the dead-or-alive Wild West?

Can it be right
not to try to hold
to the ethical high ground,
when this is the pillar
to which the Thirteen Colonies
elected to be bound?

And now?

27th April 2022, Stork

My people are coming back.
I knew they would,
before they realised it themselves.
Their dwelling lies in ruins,
a slag-heap of shattered slate,
as is the lining they use:
fabric, timber, electric cable,
but this is their place
and they will put it back,
sitting on the same location,
using whatever they can recover or adapt.

I decided to make a start of my own,
since I am their bringer of fortune,
my way of welcoming them home.
I built my nest of woven twigs
on the gable of the roofless house
in which those humans dwelled,
on which my ancestors have roosted
generation after generation,
back to the times of medieval Rus.

Aftermath

Many years on
and still alive,
but never more so
than when *they* died.

10th July 2022

In memoriam Erica Dantas Brasil

The Summer, for the moment, is warm.
Not so good if we consider what this means
in time to come.

The wars all over will go on and on,
until opposing forces reach a standstill.
Some are enriched by what this brings,
most are not,
all are gripped by fear
in varying degrees.

This is a time when hope seems scarce,
the horizon bare,
and certainty, from any dubious source,
seems preferable to where we are,
a phase in which the least disturbance
can cause the greatest harm,
with no immediate remedy in sight,
and the only thing we can do,
if we are fortunate enough,
is batten down and sit tight.

But even so, the heart of a great white whale
is six feet across and it weighs thirty stone.
When we are despairing and hopeless,
let us bask for a mile in the comfort of that.

Notes

Recovery Suite

The Covid-19 coronavirus pandemic raged from January to December 2020 without vaccines, and then long afterwards, depending on the containment and vaccination regimes implemented across the world. Until mid-2022 mask-wearing was ubiquitous in the West, much as it had been in 1918-1920 during the Spanish Flu (H1N1 influenza A) pandemic. Images of people wearing home-made masks to protect themselves from Spanish Flu were almost never seen subsequently as the horror of those years melted into the so-called Roaring Twenties.

1 'Krassimira'

Libera me
'Free me (the soul)', Giuseppe Verdi, *Messa da Requiem* (1874). The requiem was performed on September 4th, 2020 in the Piazza del Duomo, Milan by the Chorus and Orchestra of La Scala, Milan, conducted by Ricardo Chailly, in memory of the victims of Covid-19. The soprano soloist was Krassimira Stoyanova.

2 'Rivers'

los ríos / que van a dar en la mar
'the rivers / which go to flow into the sea', Jorge Manrique, *Coplas por la Muerte de su padre* ('Lines on the Death of his Father', c. 1476-1479). This late fifteenth-century elegy for Rodrigo Manrique de Lara (1406-1476), a powerful Spanish noble and military campaigner, penned by his son, Jorge, is one of the most significant and influential poems in the Spanish language.

3. 'Heaven 1918'

Als wie in der Mutter Haus
'As if in their mother's house'. The line is from 'In diesem
Wetter'/'In this Weather', by Friedrich Rückert, from
Kindertotenlieder ('Poems on the Deaths of Children'), a
collection of 563 poems he wrote in memory of the son and
daughter he lost to scarlet fever the winter of 1833-34. *In
diesem Wetter* is the fifth of five of these poems set by Gustav
Mahler (*Kindertotenlieder*, 1901-1904).

4. 'The Swan at Fuldatal'

Mo ghrá thu agus mo rún!
'You are my love and my heart's secret', Eibhlín Dubh Ní
Chonaill (1743-c.1800), *The Lament for Art O'Leary* (1773).
Eibhlín composed this lament in the days after the
assassination of her husband in Carriganima, Co Cork. Most
of it was delivered orally at his wake, funeral and burial. It is
one of the most important surviving traditional laments in the
Irish language.

Art O'Leary (Árt Ó Laoghaire, c.1747-1773) served in the
Hungarian Hussars (light cavalry) under the Empress Maria
Theresia of Austria, following a path to enlistment in the
armies of Catholic Europe trodden by many young Irish
Catholics from moneyed or noble families since the early
seventeenth century. He and a widowed Eibhlín eloped in
1767 on his return, she having been forced into marriage to a
wealthy elderly man when she was fifteen. The elopement
was in defiance of her family who were wary of Art's
reputation for recklessness and wished to see her more
conventionally re-married.

There is no certainty as to why Art was ambushed and killed. His behaviour on his return from his adventures in Austria is known to have irritated the local Church of Ireland establishment and one English-born landowner in particular. It also gave cause for concern to the few remaining members of the Irish Catholic gentry whose situation was in a permanent state of precarity under the restrictive Penal Laws (1695-1728, repealed 1771-1829). These legislated against Catholic and Dissenter alike.

The swan's plight was reported in *The Guardian* on 28th December 2020. The bird was found on the train tracks in Fuldatal, near the river Fulda in Hesse, Germany.

5. 'Forgiveness'

Elle est tout amour
'It is all love', is from the note for the eighth and final movement of the 'Quartet for the End of Time' (*Quatuor pour la fin du temps*, for violin, cello, clarinet and piano) by Olivier Messiaen (1908-1992). He refers to the song in praise of the immortality of Jesus, *Louange à l'immortalité de Jésus* which constitutes this final movement. The quartet was written while the young composer was held at a prisoner-of-war camp in Zgorzelec, on the Polish-German border. It was performed by himself and three fellow prisoners at the camp on January 15th, 1941.

The reference to the Apocalypse in the *Quatuor* is from the Book of Revelation: 'And I saw another mighty angel come down from heaven', *Revelation* 10: 1-2; 5-7, King James Version.

Statistics and Collateral Damage

'The Innocent Dead 1, Lament for a Prince of Greece'.
The funeral of H.R.H. the Duke of Edinburgh, Philip Mountbatten-Windsor, né Filippos Schleswig-Holstein-Sonderburg-Glücksberg, prince of Greece and Denmark, (10th June 1921-9th April 2021) took place under Covid restrictions at St George's Chapel, Windsor on April 17th, 2021. Three of his German great-nephews attended the funeral: the hereditary prince of Baden, the Landgrave of Hesse and the Prince of Hohenloe-Langenburg, representing the families of his four elder sisters who had all married German aristocrats. Neither his three surviving sisters nor their husbands, who had served Germany in the second world war, were invited to his wedding to the then Princess Elizabeth in 1947.

Ucrania

The scenes described here are based on images shared on Twitter in the early stages of the Russian military invasion of Ukraine, launched on February 24th, 2022. Two relate to newspaper articles, listed below.

'14th April 2022'
Seoirse Mulgrew, "Ukrainian woman (86) now living in Co. Clare reunited with her beloved dog Tasha', *Irish Independent*, 11th April 2022.

'14th May 2022'
Daniel Boffey, 'The Invisible Ukrainian', *Guardian* 13th May 2022; 'Ukrainian who walked 140 miles', *Guardian*, 15th May 2022.

Infamia

'24th May 2022, Uvalde'
At a press conference in the White House on Tuesday June 7th, the actor, Matthew McConaughy and his wife, the model Camila Alves displayed green Converse trainers like those worn by 10-year-old Maite Yulena Rodríguez who was one of those killed in the massacre at Robb Elementary School, Uvalde, Texas on 24th May. McConaughey was born in Uvalde.

'24th June 2022, The Other Side is Damnation'
The US Supreme Court overturned the Roe v. Wade ruling (1973) stipulating that abortion was a constitutional right on June 24th, 2022.

Ireland voted to legalise abortion in a referendum on 25th May 2018, after a national conversation on the question undertaken via the Citizens Assembly, a body of non-elected and randomly-selected individuals.

'31st July 2022'
The Egyptian Ayman al-Zawahiri, leader of Al-Qaeda, was assassinated by U.S. drone strike while on the balcony of his family residence in Kabul on July 31st. There were no other reported casualties.

Thirteen east-coast colonies declared independence from Britain in July 1776, constituting themselves the United States of America.

.